REDHILL
TO
ASHFORD

Vic Mitchell and Keith Smith

MP Middleton Press

Cover picture: Schools class no. 30923 Bradfield
pulls empty coaches from the siding under Tonbridge
East Box on 29th October 1958.   (J.Scrace)

First published February 1990

ISBN 0 906520 73 8

© *Middleton Press 1990*

Design and Laser typesetting -
            Deborah Goodridge

Published by Middleton Press
            Easebourne Lane
            Midhurst, West Sussex
            GU29 9AZ
            Tel. (0730) 813169

Printed & bound by Biddles Ltd,
            Guildford and Kings Lynn

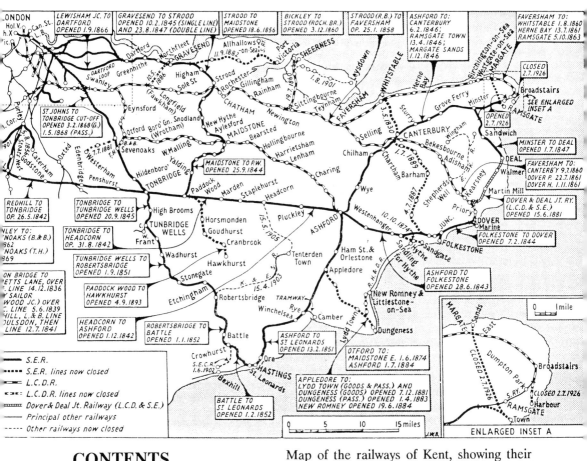

CONTENTS

Map of the railways of Kent, showing their opening dates and the pre-1899 ownership of the main lines. (Railway Magazine)

ACKNOWLEDGEMENTS

We are very grateful for the assistance received from many of the photographers noted in the credits and also for the help given by R.M.Casserley, G.Croughton, Dr.T.A.Gough, N.Langridge, J.Miller, R.Randell, N.Stanyon and our ever tolerant wives.

The gradient profile has the route mileage on the bottom line, the distances east of Tonbridge being measured from Charing Cross via Sevenoaks.

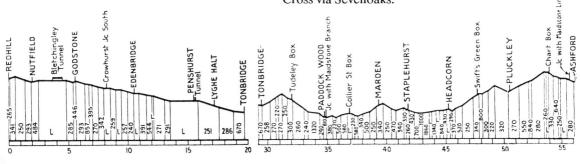

GEOGRAPHICAL SETTING

Redhill is situated in a gap in the Lower Greensand ridge which runs roughly parallel to, and at the foot of, the North Downs. The route curves onto the Weald Clay which it traverses as far as Penshurst. Tunbridge Wells Sand is then crossed, before reaching the Medway Valley, west of Tonbridge. The line follows this valley towards Paddock Wood and passes over a Medway tributary, the River Teise, between there and Marden. Another such tributary, the River Beult, is close to the railway between Staplehurst and Headcorn, from where the line is on Wealden Clay again,

until reaching the valley of the Great Stour, on the outskirts of Ashford.

The gradient falls steadily from Redhill to the Medway Valley (the total loss of height being about 170ft.), whereas east of Tonbridge the route follows an undulating course, which is almost completely straight. This unusual feature was of great navigational value to the early aviators between London and Paris, so much so that the names of some stations were painted on their roofs.

All maps in this album are to the scale of 25" to 1 mile, unless otherwise stated.

HISTORICAL BACKGROUND

The route was intended to form part of the first railway between London and Dover, the South Eastern Railway's Act being passed on 21st June 1836. From a terminus at London Bridge, trains ran over the tracks of the London & Greenwich Railway for about two miles and then on the metals of the London & Croydon Railway as far as Norwood Junction. The London & Brighton Railway built the line south from this point but the part between Stoats Nest (Coulsdon) and Redhill (then Reigate) was sold to the SER in November 1839. The SER saw this as the cheapest way to gain access to Kent and abandoned work on a tunnel at Riddlesdown, which formed part of a more direct route via Oxted.

Trains had commenced running between London and Croydon (now West) in 1839 and operated south to Haywards Heath from 12th July 1841. SER services commenced between Redhill and Tonbridge (then Tunbridge) on 26th May 1842 and were extended to Headcorn on 31st August of that year, reaching Ashford on 1st December. Operation to Folkestone commenced on 28th June 1843.

Most of the intermediate stations were opened when that part of the route came into use, the exceptions being Nutfield and Leigh

which are described in the captions.

A branch to Maidstone from Paddock Wood (then Maidstone Road) was completed on 29th September 1844.

The line from Hastings to Ashford was opened in 1851 and the direct route from Tonbridge followed in 1852.

The direct line between Tonbridge and London via Sevenoaks was ready for traffic on 1st May 1868, after which date most Dover services were transferred to this route.

On 10th March 1884, a connection to the new Oxted - East Grinstead line was opened, near Crowhurst. In the same year, the London, Chatham & Dover Railway reached Ashford from Maidstone, but a connection to the SER was not made until 1892.

At Paddock Wood, a branch south to Hawkhurst was completed in 1893 and at Headcorn a similar connection was made with the Kent & East Sussex Railway to Tenterden on 15th May 1905. These lines were closed totally on 12th June 1961 and 2nd January 1954 respectively.

Dieselisation of most local services west of Tonbridge took place in January 1965 and electrification of the eastern part of the route occurred on 12th June 1961.

PASSENGER SERVICES

The initial service was of four return trips to Tonbridge on weekdays, a Sunday train being added after a few weeks. Upon opening to Headcorn, the weekday frequency was increased to six, but this was reduced to five upon reaching Ashford.

By 1861, there were eighteen weekday journeys on the route, only five of which served the intermediate stations.

Noteworthy improvements were made on the western part of the route by the SR and again by BR when DEMUs were introduced in 1965. The latter gave a basic hourly service between Tonbridge and Reading for the first time. This lasted until May 1986, when through running largely ceased.

From then until May 1989, most trains from Tonbridge terminated at Reigate. Since electrification in 1961, the eastern half of the route has benefited from a basic hourly service, daily.

Through trains

Many local services ran through to London or the Kent Coast. When combined with the expresses between those places, they are too numerous to discuss in this summary and so the notes will be limited to long distance services operating over the entire length of the route.

A Birkenhead - Dover train ran in 1863-66 (via Reading and Redhill) but it was not until 1897 that a service from the GWR was resumed, with a Liverpool - Folkstone Harbour train.

The SR developed through running via the GWR to and from the Kent Coast, the services reaching their zenith in early years of BR, particularly on Summer Saturdays. Even during WWII, there was a train between Ashford and Newcastle, although mainly for service personnel. Prior to nationalisation in 1948, there were still four trains between London and Ashford on weekdays using the old main line via Redhill.

Regular east-west trains sadly ceased in 1964 leaving only all-station stopping trains west of Tonbridge. With the development of Ashford as a rail centre of great importance following the completion of the Channel Tunnel, maybe a regular through service to Reading will become a reality again.

Local Trains

The table below indicates the frequency of local services on the two halves of the route.

	Redhill - Tonbridge		Tonbridge - Ashford	
	Weekdays	Sundays	Weekdays	Sundays
1869	11	4	5	4
1890	10	3	9	3
1906	11	3	10	3
1914	10	3	9	3
1924	10	3	10	3
1936	16	10	9	2
1948	16	8	12	3
1959	16	9	10	2
1969	16	9	18	16

The 24 hour clock was used on BR from 14th June 1965 and so trains are thus described after that date

July 1906

REDHILL

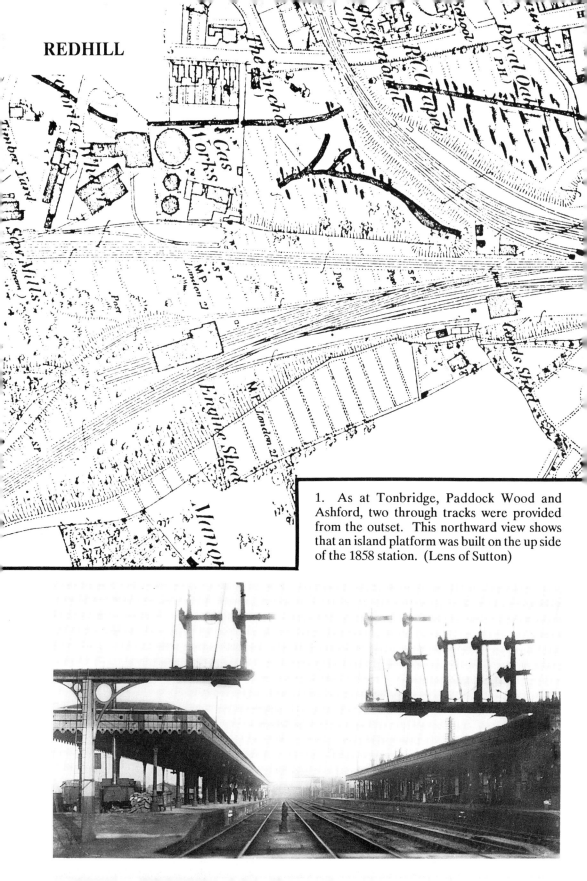

1. As at Tonbridge, Paddock Wood and Ashford, two through tracks were provided from the outset. This northward view shows that an island platform was built on the up side of the 1858 station. (Lens of Sutton)

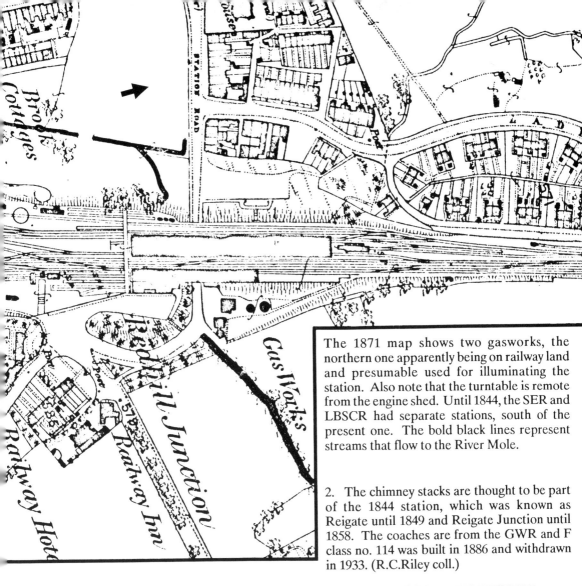

The 1871 map shows two gasworks, the northern one apparently being on railway land and presumable used for illuminating the station. Also note that the turntable is remote from the engine shed. Until 1844, the SER and LBSCR had separate stations, south of the present one. The bold black lines represent streams that flow to the River Mole.

2. The chimney stacks are thought to be part of the 1844 station, which was known as Reigate until 1849 and Reigate Junction until 1858. The coaches are from the GWR and F class no. 114 was built in 1886 and withdrawn in 1933. (R.C.Riley coll.)

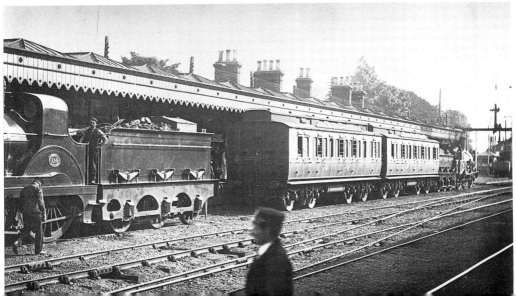

3. The main entrance was on the down side, remote from the town, and is seen before motor cars dominated the scene. The station being situated on the side of a valley, only this entrance could be at ground level.
 (Lens of Sutton)

4. Below the well-stayed through signals is the down platform starting signal and its associated semicircular route indicator. Birdcage coach no. 3463 is bound for Tonbridge behind H class no. 1276, both being ex SECR. (J.G.Sturt)

5. The 9.03am Reading to Tonbridge service snakes over the crossover behind Q class no. 30543 on 16th August 1964. The Brighton lines were completely obstructed during the operation, as testified by the up signals on the left. (R.E.Ruffell)

London Brighton & South Coast Railway.

Hayling Island to

RED HILL

6. In the reverse direction, the Brighton lines are approached by class L1 no. 31756 hauling the 9.40am Ashford to Reading, in August 1957. The locomotive shed is in the left distance. (P.Hay)

Other maps and views of this station are to be found in our *East Croydon to Three Bridges* and *Guildford to Redhill* albums, and in Peter Hay's *Steaming through Surrey.*

⟵————————

7.　On 26th February 1984, a Hastings to Charing Cross service was diverted at Tonbridge to run via Godstone and the up through road to Redhill. On the left is the Royal Mail sorting office which is connected direct to the bay platform on the left and by means of a mailbag conveyer through the covered bridge to the island platform, on the right. (P.G.Barnes)

8.　Prior to the electrification of passenger services to Reigate and to Three Bridges on 17th July 1932, the SR built this booking hall on the west side of the line. Passengers had a stiff climb to the platforms, one of the canopies being visible in the background. The building was demolished in 1989 as part of the modernisation scheme. (J.Scrace)

London Brighton & South Coast Railway.

Amberley to

Red Hill

SE&CR

ASCOT RACES

JUNE 13th, 14th, 15th and 16th, 1922.

A SPECIAL TRAIN,
WITH PULLMAN CAR ACCOMMODATION,
WILL RUN
EVERY DAY OF RACES
TO
ASCOT WEST (A few minutes from course)
AS UNDER:

As the Pullman Car accommodation is Limited, Passengers are recommended to purchase their Tickets in advance.

FROM	AT	1st CLASS, including PULLMAN CAR SUPPLEMENT. Return.	SINGLE. 1st Class. S. D.	SINGLE. 3rd Class. S. D.	RETURN. 1st Class. S. D.	RETURN. 3rd Class. S. D.
		FARES.				
EAST CROYDON	A.M. 10 40					
PURLEY	10 50					
COULSDON	10 55	**25/-**	11 10	6 0½	19 8½	10 1
MERSTHAM	11 5					
RED HILL	11 10					
REIGATE	11 20					
DORKING	11 30		11 6½	5 8½	19 8½	9 2½
CATERHAM	A 10 15	TICKETS FOR PULLMAN CAR CAN BE OBTAINED NOW AT ANY OF THE STATIONS FROM WHICH THE 25/- FARE IS QUOTED.	13 7	6 7½	22 7½	11 3
WARLINGHAM	A 10 18		13 1½	6 5½	21 10½	10 11½
WHYTELEAFE	A 10 21		13 1½	6 5½	21 10½	10 11½
KENLEY	A 10 25		12 5	6 2	20 7	10 4½
TONBRIDGE	B 10 10		18 6½	8 9½	32 6½	17 6
PENSHURST	B 10 20	REFRESHMENTS, HOT OR COLD CAN BE OBTAINED IN THE PULLMAN CARS.	17 4½	8 2½	30 6	16 4
EDENBRIDGE	B 10 28		15 11	7 6	27 10½	14 10½
GODSTONE	B 10 36		14 3½	6 9	24 8	13 5
NUTFIELD	B 10 43		12 6½	6 4	20 10½	10 8

Train Returns from Ascot West at 5.25 p.m.

A—Change at Purley ⎫ Passengers from these Stations desiring to travel by Pullman Car may do so by
B— ,, ,, Red Hill ⎬ taking an Ordinary Ticket to Purley or Red Hill, and thence re-booking.

London Bridge Station,
29 | 5 | 22.

P. C. TEMPEST, *General Manager.*

Printed by McCorquodale & Co. Ltd., London.— 16,919.

REDHILL SHED

9. A view north-east in about 1928 shows the shed in its original condition, just prior to the construction of a high level coal stage. It was common practice for shedmasters to stockpile coal at cheaper summer prices.
(Lens of Sutton)

10. Shedmasters in affluent Surrey in the prosperous 60s found difficulty in recruiting sufficient labourers for the many manual tasks in steam sheds. A shedman takes supplies to the sand furnace on 8th January 1963, during the coldest winter in living memory. A good view of the ex-SER goods shed is obtained - the LBSCR once had a separate depot further south. (R.E.Ruffell)

11. Three snow ploughs stand idle as N class 2-6-0 no. 31850 is cut up on 26th July 1964. To the left of the SR - built coaling shelter is the bridge carrying the Reigate line over the High Street. The main line to Brighton is concealed by the coal stage embankment. (S.C.Nash)

This 1933 map is an extension of the one shown below picture no. 112 in the *East Croydon to Three Bridges* album and has the Brighton line top left and the Tonbridge route lower left. The two independent stations of the LBSCR and the SER were in Hooley Lane, seen on the left of this sheet. The goods yard was formerly that of the LBSCR, the Quarry Line running parallel to it. The tunnel air shaft is marked.

→

12. From almost the same viewpoint as the previous picture, we see a sand loading siding (left of centre) and behind class Q no. 30543 is the rectangular ventilation shaft of the Quarry Line tunnel. As this bypass route to Redhill did not come into use until 1899 - 1900, it does not show on the 1871 map. (J.Scrace)

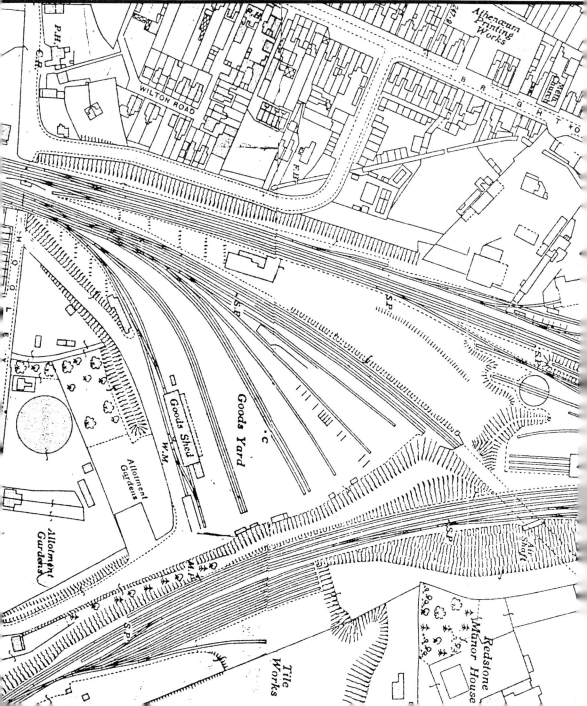

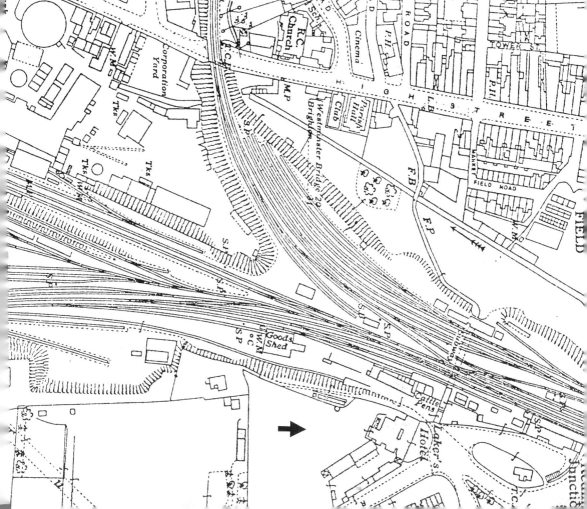

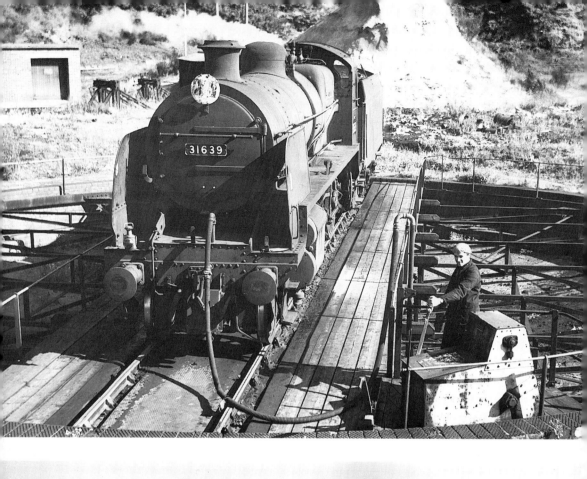

EAST OF REDHILL

upper left

13. Fireman Earlc operates the 65ft vacuum turntable, having coupled the hose to the locomotive's braking system. The table was fitted with handles for manual operation, when vacuum was not available. The photograph was taken from the end of the coal road on 4th September 1965, by which time the shed was officially closed. (R.E.Ruffell)

14. BR removed the brick arch doorways when re-roofing the shed in 1950. The eastern wall was retained when the rest of the structure was demolished and the site used for stabling diesel locomotives and multiple units. One snow plough was to be seen on 29th March 1973. (J.Scrace)

15. The main line leaves Redhill on a nine chain curve, the last curve for over seven miles. Class N no. 31864 is seen arriving with the 2.15 pm service form Tonbridge on 8th August 1959. The line in the foreground was known as the "Tonbridge siding" and, out of view on the left, there were nine sidings, extensively used for sand traffic. One was gated for the private use of Carter Wilkinson. Five remained in situ in 1989. (J.Scrace)

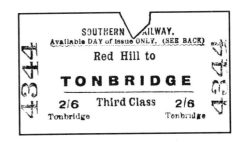

SOUTHERN RAILWAY.
Available DAY of Issue ONLY. (SEE BACK)
Red Hill to
TONBRIDGE
2/6   Third Class   2/6
Tonbridge   Tonbridge

NUTFIELD

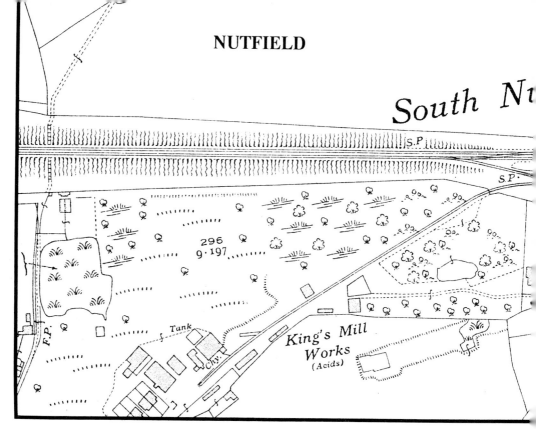

South N...

296
9·197

Tank

King's Mill
Works
(Acids)

16. The station was opened in 1883, although a public siding, known as Mid Street, had been provided here from an early date. The village is situated on the A25, one mile to the north.

This is the eastward view in 1951, the signal box remaining in use until 10th May 1970. (D.Cullum)

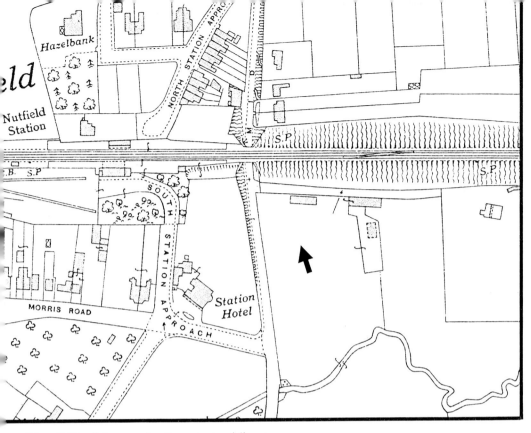

The 1937 edition marks the private siding to the chemical works of the Nutfield Manufacturing Co., which was situated on a former brickworks site.

17. Class 4 2-6-4T no. 80142 blows off in the down platform on 31st December 1964, during the last week of steam operation. In the peak hours, there were a few local workings between Redhill and Godstone. (H.N.James)

18. The architectural style was similar to that employed at Sandling Junction, which was opened five years later and where the building still remains in use. However, no footbridge was provided at Nutfield. (J.Scrace)

19. For over twenty years, the Reading - Tonbridge service was provided by Tadpole units, so nicknamed owing to a full width driving trailer being attached to two narrow vehicles, built for the London - Hastings service. DEMU no. 1202 is seen working the 11.46 from Tonbridge on 1st June 1971. (J.Scrace)

20. Goods facilities were withdrawn on 3rd January 1966; coal traffic ceased on 7th November 1966; partial staffing ended on 5th November 1967 and the buildings were subsequently demolished. Narrow - bodied class 33 no. 33208 proceeds past the permanently vandalised shelters, bound for Tonbridge on 18th June 1986. (J.S.Petley)

21. Having passed through the 1327yd. long Bletchingley Tunnel, no. 30939 *Leatherhead* speeds past William's siding with the 11.12am Charing Cross to Margate, diverted due to engineering work in Sevenoaks Tunnel, on 20th April 1952. (D.Cullum)

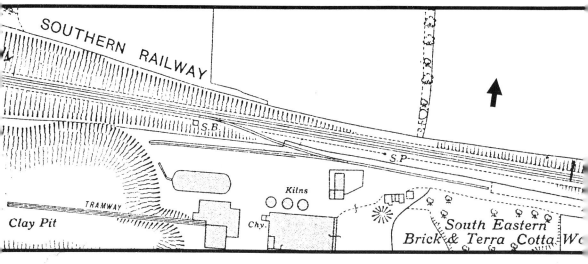

The 1937 survey indicates that the siding then served a brickworks, which had an extensive clay pit.

22. In recent years, the old clay pit has been used as the CCE's tip for spent ballast and other rubbish. Nos. 73126 and 73105 have arrived with a train from Woking on 16th November 1988. (J.Scrace)

GODSTONE

23. Between July 1914 and March 1915, the station was completely rebuilt, the platforms were raised and lengthened, and a footbridge was erected. The cattle pen in the goods yard is visible, extreme left. Romney Marsh sheep often wintered in the area and around 2000 per day were transhipped in the season in the 1930's. (D.Cullum coll.)

24. The 2.5pm from Tonbridge on 20th April 1952 was hauled by H class 0-4-4T no. 31310. The rear coach is on the points to the up siding, which could accommodate 70 wagons - the corresponding long siding on the down side could hold 65. (D.Cullum)

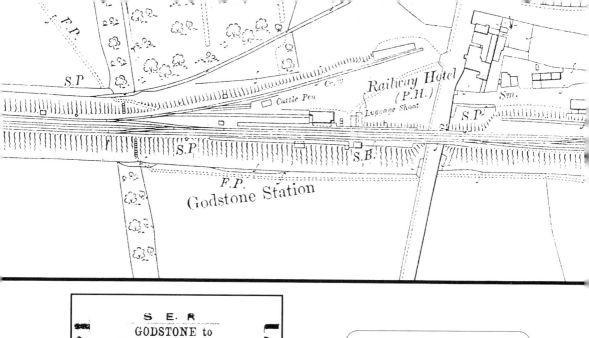

Godstone Station map showing Railway Hotel (P.H.), Cattle Pen, Luggage Shoot, S.B., S.P., F.P.

25. The signal box was in use until 1986 but the station buildings were demolished more than ten years earlier. Class 4 2-6-4T no. 80151 is seen with a Redhill - Tonbridge stopping service on 21st March 1964. (E.Wilmshurst)

Morning peak hour Redhill departures in 1959

7.06	originates
7.21	from Tonbridge
7.43	originates
8.08	originates
8.28	from Tonbridge
8.50	from Tonbridge

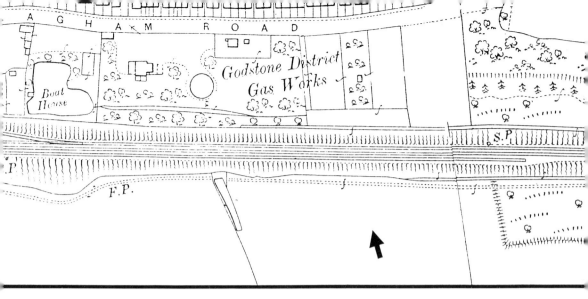

The 1912 edition marks the crane (Cr.), which was of 3 ton 7 cwt capacity, and also shows a luggage chute. East of the main road (now the A22) and on the down side is a siding known as Heasman's Wharf. The name dates back to the opening of the line when the Upper Medway Navigation made arrangements for canal borne coal to be distributed locally by the SER. They even bought their own locomotive but never gained permission for its use. The end of the long siding in the goods yard was used by another coal merchant, Varnham.

26. The wide end of Tadpole unit no. 1201 is evident as the 08.23 from Reading arrives on 2nd August 1975. Staffing of Godstone and other intermediate stations to Tonbridge ceased on 5th November 1967, when conductor guards were introduced on these trains. No evidence remains of the former buildings or goods yard, the latter having closed on 4th May 1964. Having no through services to London and being over two miles from the village, the station is now little used. (J.Scrace)

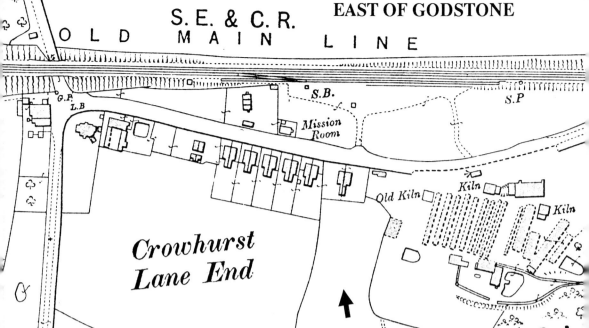

Crowhurst Lane End

Bric

Crowhurst Siding Box is situated on the up side, one mile east of Godstone station. It is marked S.B. on this 1912 survey and was closed on 22nd March 1964, although not then a block post. Part of the brickwork's quarter - mile long tramway is also evident.

27. The bridge over the Oxted - East Grinstead line is barely visible in the distance of this view towards Godstone from Crowhurst Junction South. The tracks to the right were used by only a few scheduled services between Tonbridge and London via Oxted; regular usage ceasing on 10th June 1955. The spur closed on 27th May 1965 and the box followed on 25th October. (D.Cullum)

SOUTHERN RAILWAY.
Available on DAY of Issue ONLY.
This ticket is issued subject to the By-laws, Regulations and Conditions stated in the Company's Time Tables, Bills and Notices.
Nutfield   to
CHARING CROSS
FARE 2/9   Third Class   FARE 2/9
Charing Cross   Charing Cross
2905   2905

28. D class SR no. 1748 takes the Oxted line at Crowhurst Junction South on 10th September 1950, hauling the 5.25pm Horsmonden to London Bridge hop pickers' special. The train consisted of six coaches of set 918 and four vans, the former containing hop pickers and the latter their camping equipment, much of it loaded onto perambulators. (J.J.Smith)

BRITISH RAILWAYS (S)
GODSTONE
PLATFORM TICKET 1d.
Available ONE HOUR on Day of Issue only
NOT VALID IN TRAINS. NOT TRANSFERABLE
To be given up when leaving Platform
FOR CONDITIONS SEE BACK.
9010   9010
12 11 10 9 8 7
1 2 3 4 5 6

Crowhurst Junction North Box appears in picture no. 11 of our *Branch Lines to East Grinstead.*

29. Over one mile east of Crowhurst Junction, the route passes over the Oxted - Tunbridge Wells line, the latter being in Little Browns Tunnel which is opened out at this point. A Redhill bound train is seen crossing it in 1933. (Dr.I.C.Allen)

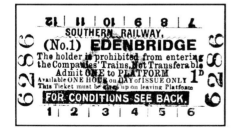

SOUTHERN RAILWAY,
(No.1) EDENBRIDGE
The holder is prohibited from entering
the Companies' Trains, Not Transferable
Admit ONE to PLATFORM 1D
Available ONE HOUR on DAY of ISSUE ONLY
This Ticket must be given up on leaving Platform
FOR CONDITIONS SEE BACK.

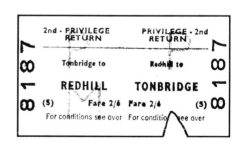

2nd - PRIVILEGE   PRIVILEGE - 2nd
RETURN   RETURN

Tonbridge to   Redhill to

REDHILL   TONBRIDGE

(S)   Fare 2/6   Fare 2/6   (S)
For conditions see over For conditions see over

30. The 1.05pm Redhill to Tonbridge train is crossing the bridge within Little Browns Tunnel on 8th October 1951, hauled by class I3 no. 32086. The road bridge carries a minor country lane. (S.C.Nash)

31. SECR 4-4-0 no. 194 approaches Edenbridge and rounds the only curve shown on the curvature diagrams between Redhill and Tonbridge. It has a 92 chain radius. (D.Cullum coll.)

EDENBRIDGE

32. The main building was on the down side and was timber framed and clad. To the right is the end loading dock and the goods shed, between which was a wagon turntable - see map. (Lens of Sutton)

33. In 1951, a SECR style rotating shunt signal was still to be found in the goods yard. Freight facilities were withdrawn on 10th September 1962. (S.C.Nash)

The 1897 map reveals a typical SER rural layout, with a pair of wagon turntables and staggered platforms. A 4-ton capacity crane was provided later.

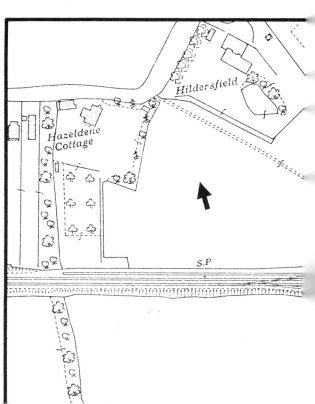

34. The foot crossing was retained after the turntables were removed and the original signal box (left) was kept (for staff purposes) when the new one was erected at the far end of the up platform. The approaching locomotive is passing the down water column - the up one was sited close to the signal box. (Lens of Sutton)

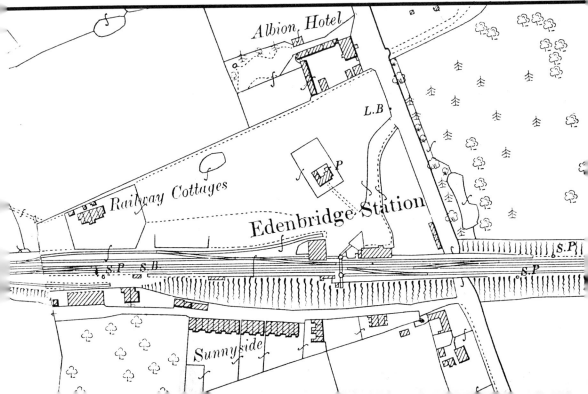

35. The 4.12pm Tonbridge to Redhill was composed of an ex-SECR Birdcage set on 8th October 1951, hauled by ex-LBSCR class I3, no. 32086. The signal box lasted until May 1986. (S.C.Nash)

36. Class 4 2-6-4T no. 80151 passes over the B2026 road bridge on 21st March 1964, while heading the 10.45am from Tonbridge. This road originated in Roman times. The town centre is one mile to the south and the population was under 4000 at that time. (E.Wilmshurst)

37. Demolition was in progress on 1st June 1971, as the motor coach of DEMU no. 1202 propels the two trailers to Tonbridge. The leading coach was usually locked, as its compartments were inaccessible to the conductor/guard. Many of the seats were missing in any case, to accommodate the heavy mail traffic. (J.Scrace)

38. Two crossovers and one siding were retained by the engineers, the control being by ground frame (right). This August 1988 photograph shows that passengers still had to cross the line on the level; that DMUs had superseded DEMUs and that a large brick-built shelter had been provided for eastbound passengers. (A.C.Mott)

PENSHURST

39. A photograph dated 1870 illustrates early SER signalling practice of a single post bearing two arms and standing close to a tiny signal cabin, located by the foot crossing. The large building in the centre background is the goods shed. (Lens of Sutton)

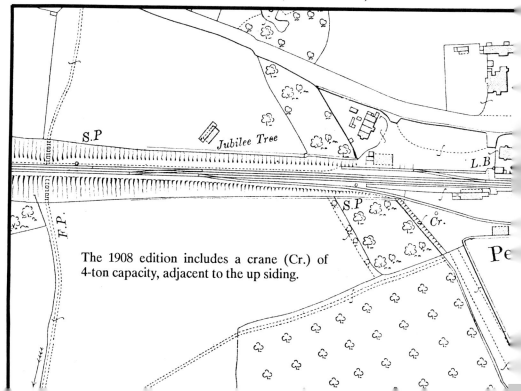

S.P

Jubilee Tree

L.B

S.P

Cr.

F.P.

Pe

The 1908 edition includes a crane (Cr.) of 4-ton capacity, adjacent to the up siding.

40. The wooden building seen in the previous photograph was fitted with a canopy, a rare occurrence on this route. The crossing was wide enough to take road vehicles requiring access to the goods shed and up siding. (Lens of Sutton)

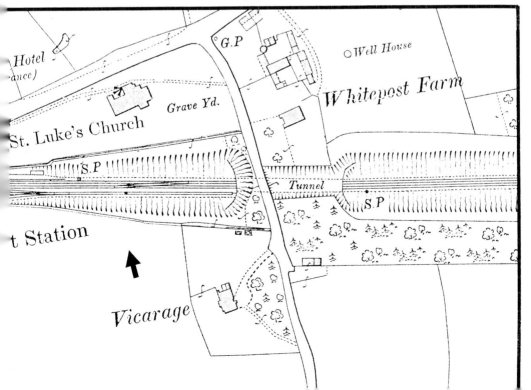

41. The signal box was built in 1893 and remained in use until 5th March 1986. The up side buildings were destroyed by fire in 1924. The station was situated in Chiddingstone Causeway, two miles north of the village of Penshurst. (Lens of Sutton)

42. The SR completed this pseudo-Tudor style station in 1925. It was photographed in 1961 and demolished about ten years later. In 1936, the RAC described Penshurst as "a bewitching old village of rare charm, with about 1600 inhabitants." (H.C.Casserley)

43. The limited visibility when shunting the goods shed is evident from the top of the tunnel in January 1952. The headshunt on the left was only 120 yards long and the siding beyond it, to the end-loading dock, was a mere 28 yds. (D.Cullum)

S. E. R. [See back.]
Available Date of issue ONLY
PENSHURST to
SELSDON ROAD
Via Edenbridge
1/7   Third   1/7
Selsdon Rd   Selsdon Rd

44. The 1.11pm from Redhill glides in behind class 4MT no. 80013 on 21st March 1964. The signal box was taken out of use on 5th March 1986 and demolished soon after. (E.Wilmshurst)

45. The goods siding ceased to be used on 9th September 1963 but two of the old shelters remained in use in 1989. This is the scene in September 1968. (J.Scrace)

46. When the railway was built, the road from Penshurst (now the B2176) was diverted away from the station site and re-routed across the top of Penshurst Tunnel. Two six-coach DEMUs from Hastings pass through the 78yd. long tunnel on 27th April 1985, bound for Penge with Girl Guides intent on celebrating the 75th anniversary of their association at Crystal Palace, despite the wintry weather. (P.G.Barnes)

LEIGH

47. A Tonbridge bound train runs in past the numerous lights of the timber built halt, which was opened on 1st September 1911. It was spelt "Lyghe Halt" between April 1917 and June 1960, but still pronounced "Lie".
(Lens of Sutton)

48. An eastward view fails to reveal the signal box, erected in 1902, to reduce the block lengths during a long period of diversion following the collapse of Chislehurst Tunnel. A similar box was built between Edenbridge and Penshurst and named Bough Beach Intermediate.
(Lens of Sutton)

49. Running bunker first, class 4 2-6-4T no. 80152 prepares to stop with the 12.45pm Tonbridge to Redhill on 21st March 1964. By then the halt had been rebuilt with concrete "harps and slabs" and fitted with gaslights.
(E.Wilmshurst)

50. When photo-graphed in 1988, the concrete posts were spalling but the village (pop. 1200 in 1936) was as beautiful as ever. A good local traffic to Tonbridge is carried - note that passengers even have the benifit of a public address system. This can be used by the Tonbridge signalman. (A.C.Mott)

4931
SOUTHERN RAILWAY.
Issued subject to the Bye-laws,
Regulations & Conditions in the
Company's Bills and Notices.
Monthly as advertised
Lyghe Halt to
PENSHURST
Third Class Fare 6½d.
NOT TRANSFERABLE
SOUTHERN RAILWAY.
MONTHLY RETURN.
Penshurst and
Lyghe Halt
Penshurst to
LYGHE HALT
Third Class Fare 6½d.
4931

51. West of Leigh, the route crosses the Medway Valley and the unsuccessful Penshurst Canal, which is chronicled by P.A.L. Vine in *Kent and East Sussex Waterways* (Middleton Press). The tranquility of the area has recently been disturbed by the new A21 trunk road. This is bridge no. 81 in January 1952. (D.Cullum)

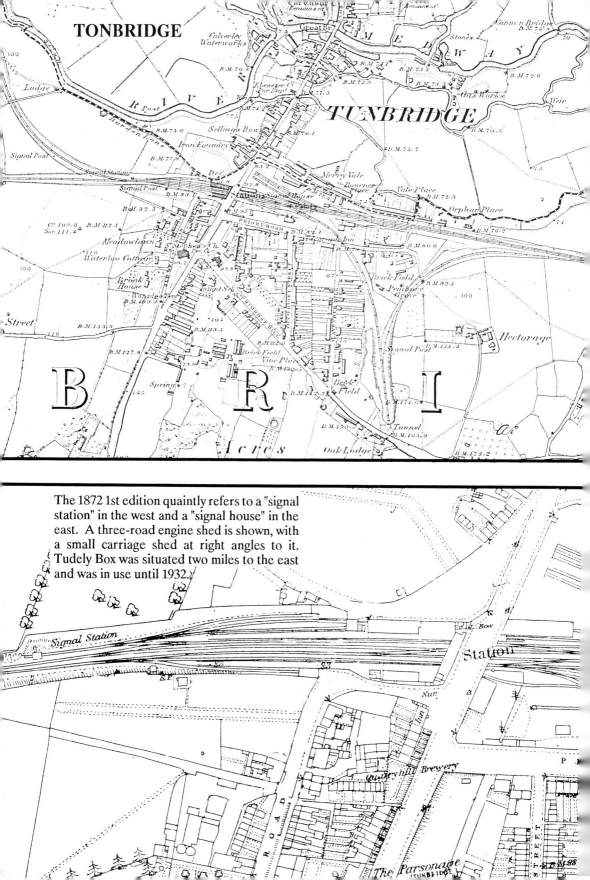

The 1872 1st edition quaintly refers to a "signal station" in the west and a "signal house" in the east. A three-road engine shed is shown, with a small carriage shed at right angles to it. Tudely Box was situated two miles to the east and was in use until 1932.

The 1889 map at 6" to 1 mile has the Redhill - Ashford route from left to right, the Sevenoaks line top left and a triangular junction for the Hastings line. The right hand part of the triangle is shown as single track and was the original route to Hastings, all trains having to reverse east of the station. This awkward procedure was due to the steep gradients involved. The direct route was added in 1857, although the original link remained until about 1913.

52. The signals surround the signal box which itself straddles the down through line. The Hastings line rises on the left of this 1870 westward view, but the platforms are just beyond the road bridge. In 1935, the box was replaced by the one seen in the cover picture. (Lens of Sutton)

Other photographs of Tonbridge can be seen in our *Tonbridge to Hastings* **album.**

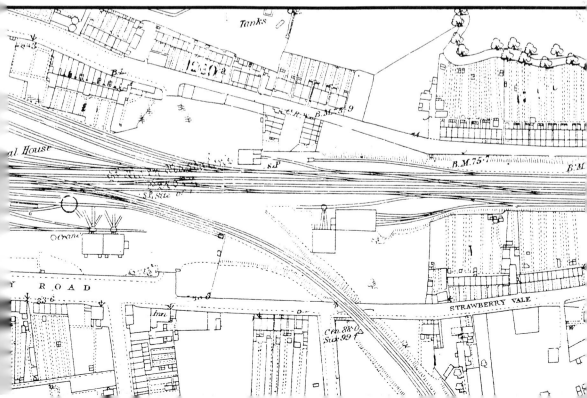

53. Seen in the background of the previous picture, the main buildings are conveniently situated at street level. Initially Tunbridge, the name was changed to Tunbridge Junction in 1852; to Tonbridge Junction in 1893 and to Tonbridge in 1929. (Lens of Sutton)

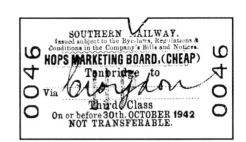

54. Although the SR was formed in 1923, this up goods train on 17th July 1926 was headed by an 0-6-0 bearing SECR livery and the number 96 on its tender. One of the signal arms bears the even earlier SER white circle, instead of a white band. One wonders why only one of the sighting boards was clean - perhaps it was new. (H.C.Casserley)

55. An impressive view from East (or A) Box shows the lines from Redhill on the right and those from Sevenoaks on the left. The box appears in the background of the next picture. (Lens of Sutton)

56. No. 77311 was one of the large number of Austerity 2-8-0s built for war service in Europe - hence the air compressor on the smokebox. It is seen on the down through line on 6th July 1946. (S.W.Baker)

57. A stopping train to Ashford stands at the down platform on 5th August 1951, apparently with a wagon, containing wheels, attached at the rear. Urgent transfer of engine parts to and from the works was sometimes achieved in this manner. H class no. 31193 is at the double sided water column. (D.Clayton)

58. The 2.15pm departure for Redhill is accelerating briskly past the West Yard, headed by H class 0-4-4T no. 31193, on 5th January 1952. The van is standing on the first of fourteen parallel sidings. (D.Cullum)

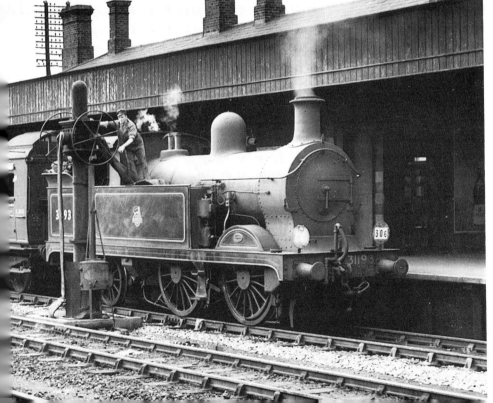

59. The headcode indicates Reading to Margate via Redhill. No. 34068 *Kenley* has its number noted by a group of "spotters" on the down platform, as it takes the through road in the summer of 1956. (Prof.H.P.White)

60. A view west from the A Box on 7th November 1960 includes the base of its successor under construction. The Redhill lines run near the left abutment of the footbridge. (British Rail)

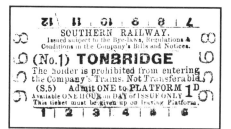

SOUTHERN RAILWAY.
Issued subject to the Bye-laws, Regulations &
Conditions in the Company's Bills and Notices.
(No.1) TONBRIDGE
The holder is prohibited from entering
the Company's Trains. Not Transferable.
(S.5) Admit ONE to PLATFORM 1D
Available ONE HOUR on DAY of ISSUE ONLY
This ticket must be given up on leaving Platform.

61. The new structure was ready to receive its panel on 16th September 1961. Unit no. 6117 stands in the berthing siding by the down Sevenoaks line, before yellow ends became obligatory and only three months after electric services had commenced. (British Rail)

62. Platform 1 ceased to be a bay on 16th June 1935 and became known as the loop. Most services from Reading terminated at it - this is the 7.45am on 2nd August 1964. (R.E.Ruffell)

63. DEMU no. 1129 forms the 16.14 departure for Edenbridge on 3rd May 1978. Behind it are two short berthing sidings for use by such units. The completed building for Tonbridge Panel is also evident. (J.Scrace)

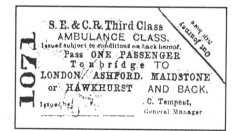

S. E. & C. R. Third Class
AMBULANCE CLASS,
Issued subject to conditions on back hereof.
Pass ONE PASSENGER
Tonbridge TO
LONDON, ASHFORD, MAIDSTONE
or HAWKHURST AND BACK.
Issued by . C. Tempest,
General Manager

1071

64. Another eastward view from the same footbridge on the same day as the previous photograph indicates that West Yard is extensively used for engineers' trains. Note that some tracks on the right are electrified. (J.Scrace)

65. Now an historical shot - the goods shed has gone, the engine has been withdrawn and the 13.45 Hoo Junction - Salfords aviation fuel train no longer runs, as a pipeline supplies the planes at Gatwick. The train ran via Maidstone West, Tonbridge and Redhill. With a 4EPB (class 415) unit in the background, no. 33045 approaches Tonbridge on 17th June 1982, ready for a change of crew. The locomotive shed once stood to the right of the last tank wagon. (J.S.Petley)

TONBRIDGE, EDENBRIDGE, REDHILL, and LONDON.

Week Days. — Up.

Miles.		mrn	mrn	mrn	mn	mrn	mrn	mrn	mrn	mrn	mrn	mrn	mrn a		aft	aft	aft	aft S
	Tonbridge..........dep.	..	6 38	.	.	7 32	..	8 38 22	..	8 59	9 28	10 38	11 8	11 38	..	12 40	..	2 13	3 6
2½	Lyghe Halt...............	..	7 4	..	.	..	..	8 108 27	..	9 5	9 33	10 43	....	11 43	..	12 45	..	2 18	3 10
4	Penshurst...............	..	7 8	..	.	7 39	..	8 148 32	..	9 10	9 38	10 48	..	11 48	..	12 49	..	2 23	3 15
9	Edenbridge ▼............	..	7 16	7 25	.	7 47	..	8 228 40	..	9 19	9 46	10 56	....	11 56	..	1257	..	2 31	3 23
14	Godstone...............	7	7 24	..	743	..	8 9	.. 8 308 48	..	9 27	9 54	11 4	..	12 5	..	1 51	542	39	3 32
17½	Nutfield...............	[290	7 13	7 31	..	749	..	8 15	.. 8 368 55	..	9 34	10 011 11	....	12 12	..	1 12	02	463	38
19½	Redhill 218, 284, arr.	7	18	7 37	..	754	..	8 20	.. 8 419 0	..	9 38	10 5	11 16	..	1136	12 18	..	1 16	2 52 513 43
30	East Croydon 284 arr.	7	45	8 9	8	F 4 827	8	F 31 8 48	....	9 69 23	..	10 11	10 38	11 46	..	12 5	12 50	..	1 47 2 51 3 18 4 4
40½	London Bridge 284 "	8	08	26	8	F 30 843	8	F 47 9 4	..	9 20	9 39	....	10 29	10 56	12 c11	..	12 31	1 11	..	2 11 3 11 3 36 4 31
37½	Clapham Junc. 284 "	8	08	23	8	F 23 9 0	8	F 32 9 10	..	9 22	....	....	10 23	....	11 c37	..	12 16	1 2	..	1 59 3 23 35 4 16
40½	Victoria 284......... "	8	7	8	28	8	F 28 9 6	8	F 57 9 16	..	9 28	9 49	....	10 29	10 57	12 d3	..	1223	1 8	..	2 5 3 8 3 42 4 23

	aft	aft	aft	aft	aft	aft	aft	aft	aft	aft	aft	aft ngt.		
	E	S	E	S	S		E					3 cl.		
Tonbridge..........dep.	4 25	4 38	5 30	5	30 5 40	..	6 16	..	7 42	8 36	9 42	10 58	12 7	..
Lyghe Halt...............	4 30	4 43	....	..	5 45	..	6 21	..	7 48	8 41	9 47	10 43	....	..
Penshurst...............	4 35	4 48	....	..	5 50	..	6 25	..	7 51	8 46	9 52	10 48	....	..
Edenbridge ▼...........	4 47	4 56	....	..	5 58	..	6 33	..	7 59	8 55	10 0	10 56	....	..
Godstone...............	5	4	5	..	5 16	6 6	10 6	4 17	28	7 9	3 10	9 11	4	..
Nutfield...............	5	4	3 11	..	5 38	6 13	6 16	6 47	7	8 8	5 14	9 10	1016	1111	....	..
Redhill 218, 284, 290.. arr.	5	10	5 18	5 58	6	46	186	21	6 527	13 8	19	9 15	1021	1116	1236	..
East Croydon 284...... "	5	50	5 50	6 29	6	26	6 50	6	51 7	18 7	51 8	47	9 48	10 48	1147	1259	..
London Bridge 284.... "	6	7	6 11	6 48	6	47 7	11 7	11 7	36 8	11 9	11	1012	1111	1213	1620	..
Clapham Junction 234. "	6	2	..	..	7	27	2	..	8	20	6 10	1 11	1 1159	....	..
Victoria 284......... "	6	15	6	8	6 57	6 57	7	87	87	8	89	6 10	711	712	5	....	..

S or § Saturdays only.   ▼ 1 mile to Edenbridge Town Station.

a	Through Train Margate to G.W. Line via Reading, see pages 330a. and 290, also to Bournemouth via Guildford, see page 290.	
c	Arr. 12 3 aft. on Sats	
d	Arr. 12 11 aft. on Sats.	
E	or § Except Saturdays.	
F	Via Oxted, see page 245.	
H	Cannon Street.	

Sundays. — Up.

	mrn	mrn	mrn		aft	aft	aft	aft	aft	ngt.	
Tonbridge..........dep.	8 35	9	7 10	35	..	2 10 6	5 7	2 1 8	12 10	1 12	7	..
Lyghe Halt...............	8 40	9	12 10	40	..	2 15 6	10 7	26 8	18 10	8 5 d..	..
Penshurst...............	8 44	9	17 10	45	..	2 19 6	16 7	31 8	23 10	13 ..	..
Edenbridge ▼...........	8 52	9	25 10	53	..	2 27 6	25 7	40 8	31 10	21 ..	..
Godstone...............	9	0	9 33	11	1	..	2 35 6	33 7	48 8	39 10	29 ..	..
Nutfield...............	9	7	9 39	11	8	..	2 42 6	40 7	55 8	46 10	36 ..	..
Redhill 222, 285, 291..	9	12	9 44	11	13	..	2 47 6	45 8	0 8	51 10	41 1236	..
East Croydon 285 ......arr.	9	35	10	4	11	46	..	3	4 7	4 8	2 49	2 11	4 1259	....
London Bridge 288 "	..	1010	1035	12	10	..	3 35	7	35 8	48 10	2 11	52 1520	....
Clapham Junction 288 "	..	..	1016	11	59	..	3 16	7	16 8	50 9	39 11	16	..
Victoria 285.......... "	9	54	10 22	12	5	..	3 22	7	22 8	56 9	46 11	42	..

H Cannon Street.

▼ 1 mile to Edenbridge Town Station.

August 1934

TONBRIDGE SHED

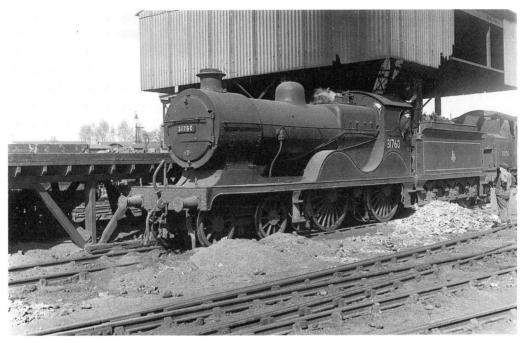

66. The asbestos cladding of the coal stage was no longer perfect when nos. 31760 and 80150 were alongside on 24th May 1958. A shed on this site housed 30 engines at the end of the SER era and 50 by the beginning of WWII. (J.Scrace)

67. The east end of the shed is seen on 22nd April 1961, in the presence of Q1 class no. 33030 and C class no. 31244, the main water tank also being visible. The new roof and gable ends date from 1952. Ten years later, the allocation was down to ten engines, closure taking place in June 1964, although diesels continued to be berthed nearby. (J.Scrace)

PADDOCK WOOD

68. The promoter's ideals of speed and punctuality are well illustrated by the provision of through roads and a clock on the tower, on the right of this 1872 photograph. Until the branch to Maidstone was opened on 29th September 1844, the station was aptly named Maidstone Road. (Lens of Sutton)

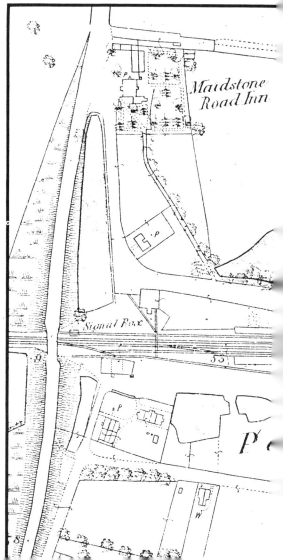

The cartographer of the 1st edition (circa 1865) has failed to mark the wagon turntables. The woodland north-east of the station was all that remained of the original Paddock Wood by then.

69. Looking over the parapet of the road bridge, "Paddock Wood West Yard Signals" is seen on the left, while the roof of the East Box is visible in the distance. The great height of the box on the left enabled the signalman to see over the road embankment. (Lens of Sutton)

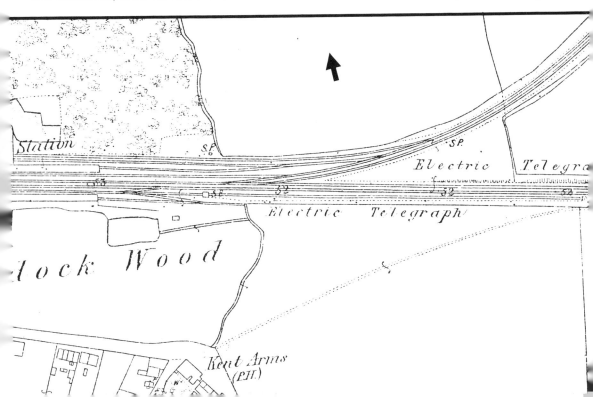

70. The up side was rebuilt in 1893 and a new footbridge, together with canopies for both platforms, were provided later. Sundry sheds and other buildings were added over the years. (Lens of Sutton)

72. A 1957 view of an up express includes part of the original goods shed, on the extreme left. Cattle pens are to be seen to the left of the locomotive. On the right is the entrance to Top Yard - all the goods yards closed to general traffic on 3rd January 1966. (Prof.H.P.White)

71. The vans behind O1 class no. 31370 obscure the Maidstone branch, as it takes the up through road on 9th August 1952. The row of cattle trucks emphasises the importance of the junction in the life of the surrounding rural community. (H.C.Casserley)

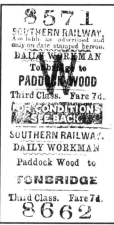

73. Bearing "The Man of Kent" headboard, Schools class no. 30910 *Merchant Taylors* speeds east with a good clear exhaust, on 27th June 1959. The train is the 4.15pm Charing Cross to Margate, via Dover. In the up bay is H class 0-4-4T no. 31239, with a Hawkhurst train. (E.Wilmshurst)

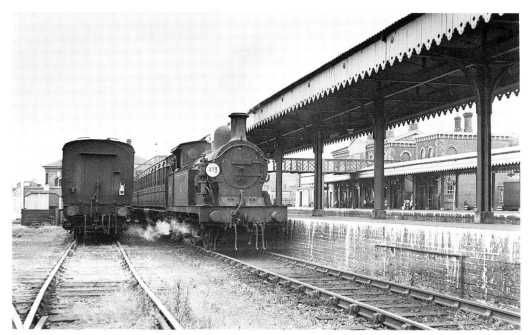

74. A closer look at the Hawkhurst train on the same day shows the collection of hoses necessary for push-pull working. There were six departures on weekdays until the branch closed on 12th June 1961. (E.Wilmshurst)

75. An up stopping train ambles into the loop behind no. 34068 *Kenley* on 9th June 1961, three days before electric traction was introduced. The signal box closed on 1st April 1962, having taken over the work of A Box (at the other end of the station) on 26th June 1932. Tonbridge Panel now controls the area. (T.Wright)

76. A look westwards on 3rd February 1983 shows that there is a siding beyond the road bridge. This is fitted with conductor rail and earlier it was paralleled by Hernden siding. Electro-diesel no. 73139, with its collector shoes lowered, is propelling a guards' training special. (J.S.Petley)

77. The Transfesa Continental Freight Terminal was opened in 1973, the shed containing three tracks and 106 loading bays. With Paddock Wood station in the background, no. 33052 *Ashford* departs at 11.22 on 20th August 1982 with vans from the Transfesa Terminal and bound for mainland Europe, via the train ferry from Dover. (J.S.Petley)

78. A special from Victoria to Dover Western Docks races along the down through road on 21st October 1988, the leading unit being no. 1521 and one of a batch refurbished with the hardest seats on BR (in the opinion of your bony author, V.M.). The adjacent down loop is now signalled for reversible running, enabling up trains to start from platform 2. (J.Scrace)

79. The up side building has been re-roofed and otherwise modernised and the delightful and unusual gate to the former goods yard has been retained (right). The long footbridge has lost its roof and can be seen passing through a gap in the up platform canopy. (V.Mitchell)

80. Another photograph from 27th May 1989 shows DMU no. L841 providing an emergency service to Ashford, due to a broken conductor rail. The bus was in the station yard for the same reason. Platform 3 (right) is used for the hourly service to Strood, via Maidstone West. (V.Mitchell)

Further details of this station can be obtained from our *Branch Line to Hawkhurst*, the first ten pictures of which feature this location.

81. An intermediate block post was provided two miles east of Paddock Wood, until 27th January 1962. Collier Street Box is seen in 1955, when flat bottom rails were being introduced in the vicinity. (J.J.Smith)

MARDEN

82. An 1890 view towards Paddock Wood includes the 1876 down building on the right. This contained a waiting area, a store and a lamp room, at the far end. The round end to the wagon was designed to support tarpaulin sheets. (Lens of Sutton)

The 1897 survey indicates three sidings in the goods yard. A fourth was added by 1908, south of the crane, which was of 3 - ton capacity. The down siding was lengthened to 204 yards, almost to the road bridge.

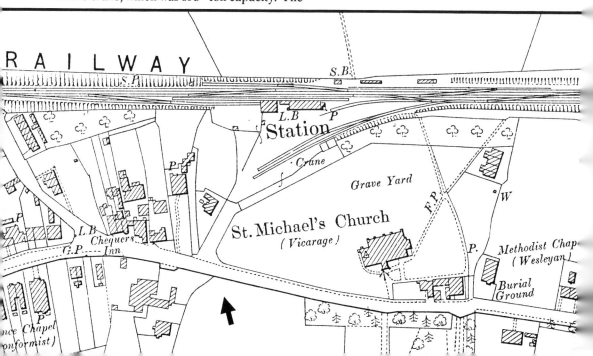

83. The main building, on the right, has casement windows which were later changed to the sash type, as fitted to the signal box. Note the additional shelter on the down platform. (Lens of Sutton)

84. The goods shed was unusual in that wagons could not pass through it. The later addition of a wooden goods office (right) was more common. The down siding (left) had no road access and was for storage only. (Lens of Sutton)

85. Toilet facilities were a nameless afterthought (right). Stacks of fruit baskets in the goods yard are a reminder that Marden was surrounded by orchards, which gave rise to an immense seasonal rail traffic. (Lens of Sutton)

87. The exterior, in 1979, retained its letter box near the door for parcels (left). Apart from re-roofing in asbestos, little had changed. The nearby village has grown recently, but its population was little over 2000 between the wars. (D.Cullum)

86. Conductor rails are in position, although temporarily lowered to permit continued use of the foot and barrow crossing. Associated with the electrification scheme was the lengthening of the platforms of most of the intermediate stations. (Prof.H.P.White)

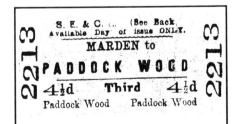

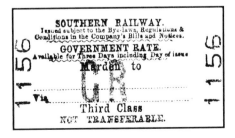

88. The advent of NSE brought about a total rebuild and further platform improvements, although the concrete footbridge dates from 1961. The second bridge carries a public footpath. The number of commuter, or "daily breaders" as they were once known, has increased steadily. (J.Scrace)

89. A second picture from October 1988 reveals the pleasing traditional exposed timberwork internally and that the letterbox has been replaced in the south elevation. (J.Scrace)

90. An early postcard shows that while one of the wagon turntables was retained (left of centre) the track across the main lines had been removed. This view is from the road bridge, looking towards Marden, with the doubled gabled warehouse on the left and the goods shed beyond it. (Lens of Sutton)

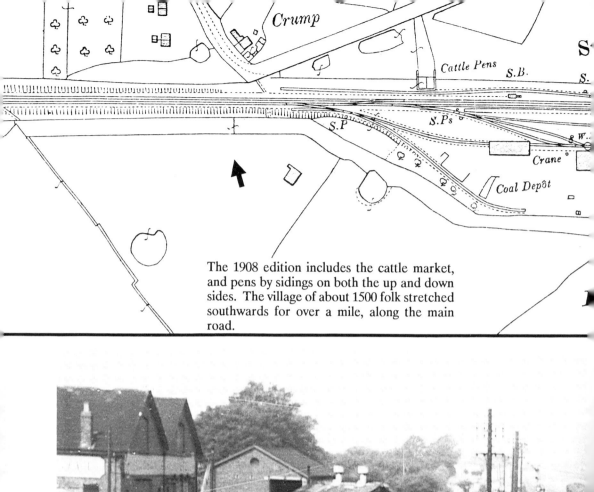

Crump

Cattle Pens

S.B.

S.P

S.Ps

Crane

Coal Depôt

The 1908 edition includes the cattle market, and pens by sidings on both the up and down sides. The village of about 1500 folk stretched southwards for over a mile, along the main road.

91. From the same viewpoint, but about 50 years later, no. 35001 *Channel Packet* hurries towards Ashford. This locomotive caused a sensation upon its first appearance, as it was the first of the revolutionary bright green "spam cans". A coal concentration depot was established here in September 1965 but all freight facilities were withdrawn on 4th October 1971. (Prof.H.P.White)

92. The locomotive water tank is close to the A229 bridge, the down column being at the far end of the platform (beyond the bridge) and the up column being beyond the signal box - see previous picture. Platform lengthening is in progress, prior to electrification.
(Lens of Sutton)

94. On the night of 21st January 1960, the up side buildings were destroyed by fire - the replacement is seen on the right of this August 1988 photograph, which also includes its new successor. The footbridge dates from 1961. (J.Scrace)

93. The SER did not provide balconies to facilitate window cleaning - just a ladder. A siding had once run behind the box to reach the cattle pens on the left. The box was replaced by a new one on 1st April 1962, it being incorporated within the station buildings. (Lens of Sutton)

3rd - SINGLE   SINGLE - 3rd
Staplehurst to
Staplehurst   Staplehurst
Cannon St. or Lon. B'dge   Cannon St. or Lon. B'dge
CANNON STREET or LONDON BRIDGE
via Chelsfield
(S)   6/-   FARE 6/-   (S)
For conditions see over   For   tions see over

2227   2227

HEADCORN

95. The entire staff appears to be posing in this classic view from about 1880. Goods traffic was given more extensive and substantial accommodation than passengers at such rural stations, as it was often the greater source of revenue. (Lens of Sutton)

The 1897 layout was similar to others on the SER, a noteable feature being the four railway cottages. The crane could lift four tons.

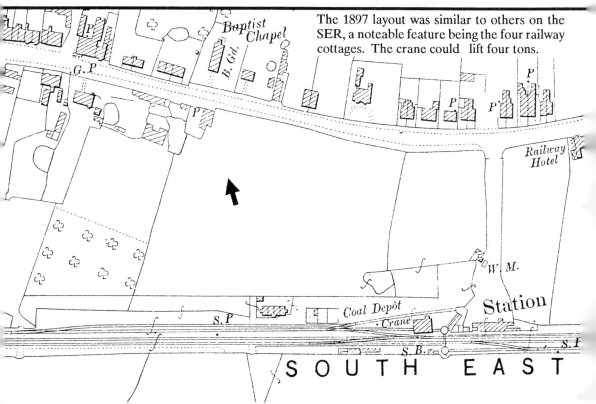

96. On 15th May 1905, the independent Kent & East Sussex Railway commenced services to Tenterden and Robertsbridge. Only that company described the station as "Headcorn Junction". SR locomotives were often hired, but class O1 no. 1064 is seen soon after the line was taken over by BR in 1948. (Lens of Sutton)

97. Although the tender bears the word SOUTHERN, the C class 0-6-0 had received a BR number (31277), when photographed on the down loop on 2nd July 1949. The loops had been completed in 1930, the old up line becoming the down through - note the kink in the distance. (H.C.Casserley)

98.The quadrupling through the station necessitated the provision of a new platform for the KESR (right). Picture no. 113 in our *Branch Line to Tenterden* shows the original arrangement, when the KESR had a straight platform parallel to the SECR up platform. South of Tenterden, steam trains now operate again in the summer and on most weekends throughout the year. (D.Cullum)

99. A new signal box was built, as its predecessor had to be demolished during the widening. The connection with the KESR was moved from the east to the west of the station at this time. The wagons on the right are standing on it, as L class no. 31772 races past with the 11.30am Ramsgate to Charing Cross on 20th April 1956. (C.Saunders)

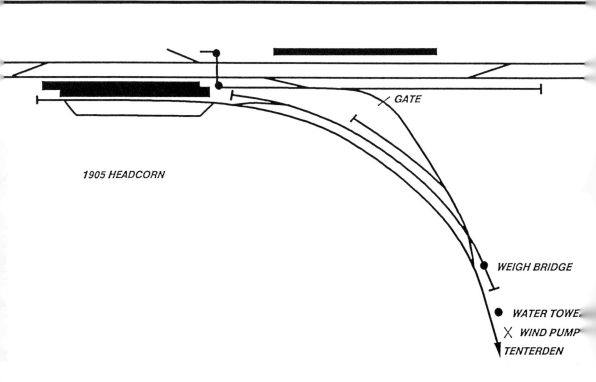

1905 HEADCORN

GATE

WEIGH BRIDGE

● WATER TOWER

X WIND PUMP

▼ TENTERDEN

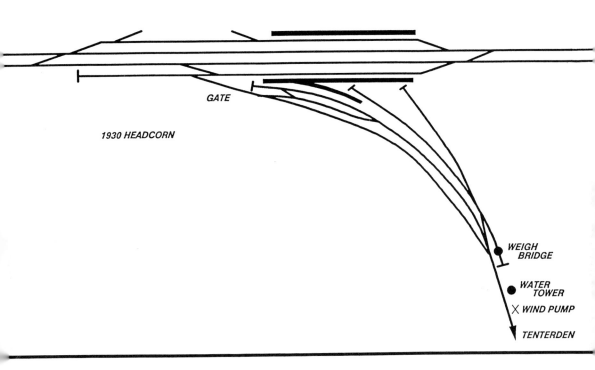

GATE

1930 HEADCORN

WEIGH BRIDGE

● WATER TOWER

✕ WIND PUMP

TENTERDEN

100. Electrification did not mean the end of locomotive haulage, as is seen on 3rd March 1962 when no. E5021 headed the down "Golden Arrow", complete with flags and bodyside arrows. (S.C.Nash)

101. The old buildings were demolished in
November 1988, the signal box having closed
on 28th July 1968 and freight facilities having
been withdrawn on 2nd April 1962. This is the
scene in November 1986. (J.Scrace)

102. A building with some character was
erected and officially opened by Miss Ann
Widdicombe MP on 11th May 1989. This
photograph was taken two weeks later.
(V.Mitchell)

103. The "Golden Arrow" always presented a
stirring sight with its all-Pullman train and a
consistently immaculate locomotive. On 25th
March 1961, it was no. 34100 *Appledore* that
was speeding towards the coast, past Swifts
Green Signals, and climbing at 1 in 340. The
box was nearly three miles west of Pluckley and
closed on 27th January 1962. (J.J.Smith)

BRITISH RLYS.(S)   BRITISH RLYS.(S)
Privilege Single   Privilege Single
Valid 3 Days   Valid 3 Days
Headcorn to
Headcorn   Headcorn
Ashford (K't)   Ashford (K't)
ASHFORD (KENT)
THIRD CLASS   THIRD CLASS
FOR CONDITIONS   FOR CONDITIONS
SEE BACK   SEE BACK
0515

SOUTHERN RAILWAY.
This ticket is issued subject to the Company's
Bye-laws, Regulations and Conditions in their
Time Tables, Notices and Book of Regulations.
Available on DAY of issue ONLY.
Headcorn to
Headcorn   Headcorn
Staplehurst   Staplehurst
STAPLEHURST
THIRD CLASS   THIRD CLASS
Fare 5½d.   Fare 5½d.
6316

PLUCKLEY

104. An 1874 photograph features the tiny signal cabin, solitary signal, exposed rafter ends, wide boarding, casement windows and painted fence boards. (Lens of Sutton)

The 1908 map marks the position of the 5 ton crane and the gate across the private siding to the brickworks.

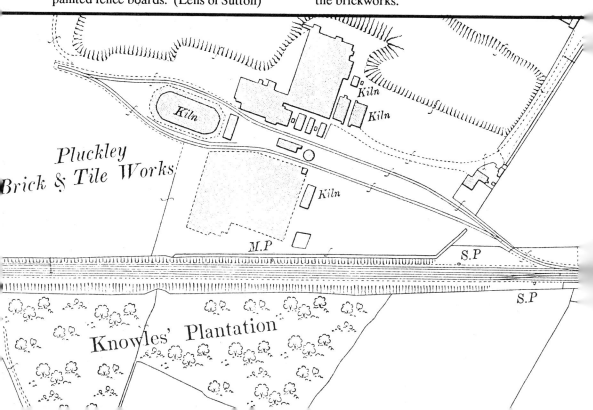

105. As at other stations on the line, it received a large signal box, full signalling, wider barge boards, narrower cladding boards, sash windows and creosoted fencing. This and the next two photographs were taken in June 1958. (H.C.Casserley)

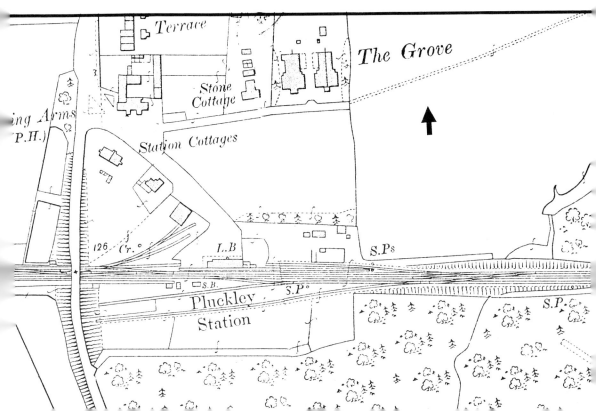

106. The goods yard closed on 20th September 1965 and the signal box followed on 17th December 1967. The gloom and the rain makes recognition of L class no. 31767 difficult. (H.C.Casserley)

107. The north elevation includes a surface mounted letterbox and a small canopy, similar to those on other stations on the route. The station master's house is on the right and the station remained unaltered in 1989. (H.C.Casserley)

108. No. 47557 hauls coaches of assorted colours forming the 07.40 Manchester to Dover Western Docks train on 23rd April 1988. From the following May, the frequency was reduced to one a day, running via Chatham and not Ashford. More publicity is needed for these useful through services. (J.S.Petley)

109. The end of the public siding at Chart, two miles from Ashford, is seen on 8th April 1961, as an up train is signalled. The signal box was a block post and closed on 29th April 1962. Known as a "road siding", this facility was located half a mile north of Great Chart Church. (J.J.Smith)

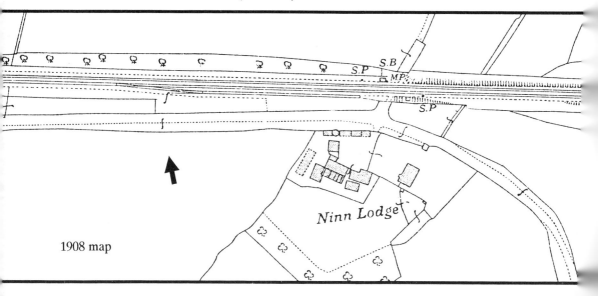

1908 map

110. One mile west of Ashford, a new carriage repair shop and inspection shed was built on the up side in 1960-61 and a third track was laid from the station to give access independent of the main lines. One of the 24 electric locomotives is visible on 28th June 1975. (R.E.Ruffell)

111. The junction with the former LCDR route to Maidstone East is seen from an up train on 20th July 1957. That railway initially had its own independent terminus behind the signal box. The latter closed on 29th April 1962, when Ashford Panel came into use. (A.E.Bennett)

ASHFORD

112. An unusually low view of the up through platform includes the roof over the up bay (left) and the four brick arches of the road bridge, so similar to those still existing at Tonbridge. (Lens of Sutton)

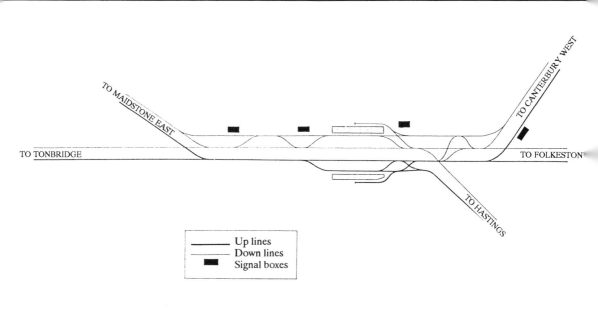

113. A camera on the footbridge gives a good impression of the extent of the station and includes the roofs of the locomotive works in the distance. The goods train in the down through platform appears to include two engines out of steam, which were probably on their way to the works. (Lens of Sutton)

Layout in the vicinity of Ashford Station before and after the alterations of 1961-62. (Railway Magazine).

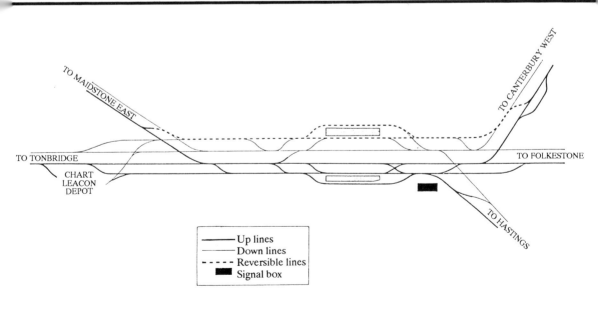

TO MAIDSTONE EAST

TO CANTERBURY WEST

TO TONBRIDGE

TO FOLKESTONE

CHART LEACON DEPOT

TO HASTINGS

———— Up lines
———— Down lines
- - - - Reversible lines
▬▬ Signal box

114. Ashford also had a carriage works, which is why P class no. A178 was shunting carriage underframes. This 1929 picture includes the down platform refreshment room and a horse box (with a groom compartment) in the down bay. This locomotive is now on the Bluebell Railway. (J.A.G.Coltas)

115. King Arthur class no. E771 *Sir Sagramore* roars through on the down fast road on 17th October 1929, while H class 0-4-4T no. A329 stands in the up loop. The SR used these prefix letters to refer to engines of Eastleigh or Ashford origin, but changed the system to numbers in June 1931. (H.C.Casserley)

116. D Box had a river on both flanks but the bridges are not obvious to travellers, owing to the large number of tracks at this location. The down starting signals are featured as N class no. 31405 takes the up through line in the summer of 1957. (F.W.Ivey)

117. The down side buildings had been much mutilated by the time they were photographed in 1958. Many additions disfigured them - the patched brickwork indicates the site of the former footbridge. (Prof.H.P.White)

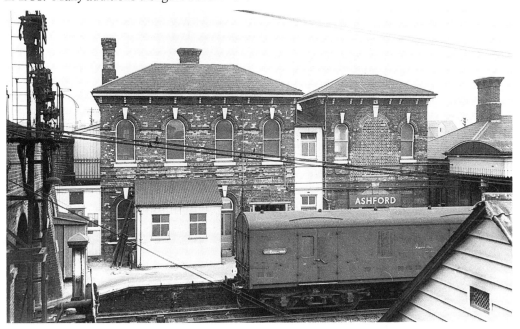

118. The opposite side of the building contained the parcels entrance in 1958. The main entrance for passengers is under the canopy and D Box is in the distance.
(Prof.H.P.White)

Other maps and pictures are included in *Hastings to Ashford* and *Ashford to Dover*. Peter Hay's *Steaming Through Kent* includes other views of the route from Edenbridge.

119. No. 47594 heads the 07.49 Liverpool to Dover Western Docks as it approaches Ashford station on 6th November 1986, two years after the first major track improvements since electrification in 1961. Through trains are now permitted to run at 85 mph. (J.Scrace)

120. DEMU no. 205002 stands in the up loop, having arrived from Hastings, while no. 205012 is on the up slow line, ready to return there on 25th August 1988. EMU no. 1547 is on the down fast road, operating a special service from Victoria to Dover Western Docks. Prior to electrification, the station was rebuilt and the bay platforms extended to form loops. The station is thus able to cope with the regular traffic converging from five routes and is poised ready to handle the increased traffic from the Channel Tunnel. New track work is to be provided and an £80m resignalling scheme includes a new panel at Ashford. (J.Scrace)

```
 ┌──────────────────────────────────┐
 │   S E. & C.        SEE BACK)      │
2│  Available Day of Issue ONLY      │2
8│                                   │8
3│        Ashford to                 │3
2│                                   │2
 │     T O N B R I D G E             │
N│  2/2½ Third Class 2/2½            │N
 │   Tonbridge          Tonbridge    │
 └──────────────────────────────────┘
```

Middleton Press

Easebourne Lane, Midhurst. West Sussex. GU29 9AZ
(0730) 813169

BRANCH LINES

BRANCH LINES TO MIDURST
BRANCH LINES AROUND MIDHURST
BRANCH LINES TO HORSHAM
BRANCH LINES TO EAST GRINSTEAD
BRANCH LINES TO ALTON
BRANCH LINE TO HAYLING
BRANCH LINE TO SOUTHWOLD
BRANCH LINE TO TENTERDEN
BRANCH LINES TO NEWPORT
BRANCH LINES TO TUNBRIDGE WELLS
BRANCH LINE TO SWANAGE
BRANCH LINES TO LONGMOOR
BRANCH LINE TO LYME REGIS
BRANCH LINE TO FAIRFORD
BRANCH LINE TO ALLHALLOWS
BRANCH LINES AROUND ASCOT
BRANCH LINES AROUND WEYMOUTH
BRANCH LINE TO HAWKHURST
BRANCH LINES AROUND EFFINGHAM JNC

SOUTH COAST RAILWAYS

CHICHESTER TO PORTSMOUTH
BRIGHTON TO EASTBOURNE
RYDE TO VENTNOR
EASTBOURNE TO HASTINGS
PORTSMOUTH TO SOUTHAMPTON
SOUTHAMPTON TO BOURNEMOUTH
ASHFORD TO DOVER
BOURNEMOUTH TO WEYMOUTH

SOUTHERN MAIN LINES

HAYWARDS HEATH TO SEAFORD
EPSOM TO HORSHAM
CRAWLEY TO LITTLEHAMPTON
THREE BRIDGES TO BRIGHTON
WATERLOO TO WOKING
VICTORIA TO EAST CROYDON
TONBRIDGE TO HASTINGS
EAST CROYDON TO THREE BRIDGES
WOKING TO SOUTHAMPTON
WATERLOO TO WINDSOR
LONDON BRIDGE TO EAST CROYDON

COUNTRY RAILWAY ROUTES

BOURNEMOUTH TO EVERCREECH JNC
READING TO GUILDFORD
WOKING TO ALTON
BATH TO EVERCREECH JUNCTION
GUILDFORD TO REDHILL
EAST KENT LIGHT RAILWAY
FAREHAM TO SALISBURY
BURNHAM TO EVERCREECH JUNCTION
REDHILL TO ASHFORD

LONDON SUBURBAN RAILWAYS

CHARING CROSS TO DARTFORD

STEAMING THROUGH

STEAMING THROUGH KENT
STEAMING THROUGH EAST HANTS
STEAMING THROUGH SURREY
STEAMING THROUGH WEST SUSSEX
STEAMING THROUGH THE ISLE OF WIGHT
STEAMING THROUGH WEST HANTS

OTHER RAILWAY BOOKS

WAR ON THE LINE
GARRAWAY FATHER & SON
LONDON CHATHAM & DOVER RAILWAY
INDUSTRIAL RAILWAYS OF THE S. EAST
WEST SUSSEX RAILWAYS IN THE 1980S

OTHER BOOKS

MIDHURST TOWN THEN & NOW
EAST GRINSTEAD THEN & NOW

WALKS IN THE WESTERN HIGH WEALD

MILITARY DEFENCE OF WEST SUSSEX
SUSSEX POLICE FORCES

SURREY WATERWAYS
KENT AND EAST SUSSEX WATERWAYS